What is PTSD?

By Brandon Burke

DeeJak's Publishing Company
Charlotte, North Carolina
www.deejakspublishing.com

DeeJak's Publishing Company
7209- J East WT. Harris Blvd # 279
Charlotte, NC 28227-1004
www.deejakspublishing.com

Editorial: Micheal Furham
Cover design by: Brandon Burke
Layout Design by: Crystal Jeffrey
ISBN: (softcover) 978-0-9857903-6-3
Library of Congress Control Number: 2014947548
Because of the dynamic nature of the Internet, any web addresses or links contained in this book may have changed since publication and may no longer be valid. The views expressed in this work are solely those of the author and do not necessarily reflect the views of the publisher, and the publisher here by disclaims any responsibility for them.

What Is PTSD?

Written & Illustrated By

Brandon Burke

6

Dedication

For Savannah and Hunter, you guys are everything

good in my life.

For my wife thank you for your love and support. This book

would not have been possible without your encouragement.

This book is dedicated to all of those who served

and never really came home.

"Stay Frosty."

Respectfully,

Larry Brandon Burke, Sergeant, USMC (1998-2005)

Isis, you are the tip of the spear for me my friend, good girl.

Hello!

My name is Lucas.

I like to play and have fun.

Sigh ...

That's my daddy's PTSD, and it's in a
bad mood.

It likes to stomp around and growl at everything that upsets it.

PTSD likes to sit on my daddy's shoulder and wait for him to be in a large crowd or a tough situation that triggers a memory of something that he has seen or done. Then it likes to make the situation worse by making him feel nervous or upset.

When my daddy least expects it, PTSD pops up just to cause him trouble.

It doesn't like to have fun or play. PTSD just wants to be angry all the time.

PTSD likes to tell daddy that it isn't real and then it causes him to get upset over things that normally would not bother him.

It always, always, always makes things worse!

But PTSD is very real.

It is not a joke.

It is usually caused when a person goes through a scary situation that they relive through their memories and dreams.

PTSD (Post Traumatic Stress Disorder) is always looking for a fight when it's mad.

PTSD can be embarrassing sometimes. Like the time it yelled at a total stranger for cutting in line for a ride that we weren't even going on!

It even tries to scare the dog!

Sometimes it likes to cause trouble and break things that belong to others.

PTSD is always looking for trouble.

But my daddy didn't always have PTSD. It was caused by things he experienced when he was in the military.

My daddy decided to go see a special doctor called a "psychiatrist" to get some help. He told my daddy that his PTSD was a manageable problem and with the proper treatment and counseling, he would be able to get it under control.

He even got a special dog called a "PTSD Service Dog" to help him keep his PTSD in check so it wouldn't cause trouble any more.

The dog helps my daddy by being by his side and watching out for him.

When she senses his anxiety level go up, she helps by "blocking" for him. Which means she gets between him and other people and leans against him.

You want to know if this really works?

Well, lets just say she is really good at her job.

My daddy's service dog keeps his PTSD on the run!

Since my daddy got help and an awesome service dog that helps keep his PTSD under control, we can go play anytime we want.

Questions

1. What is PTSD?

PTSD means Post Traumatic Stress Disorder and it is an illness.

2. What causes PTSD?

PTSD is caused by traumatic experiences.

3. Who can help with PTSD?

Psychiatrists who are specially trained.

4. What kind of animal can help with PTSD?

Dogs trained to be PTSD Service Dogs.

5. When someone with PTSD gets upset is it anybody's fault?

No, it isn't.

6. What do PTSD Service Dogs do for their owners?

They provide comfort and security to their owners in situations that cause them to feel anxious or upset.

Special Thanks to:

Jerry and Denise Kiah of Vom KiaHaus
Working German Shepherds
"Thank you for one fine girl, she's a best friend
like no other."

Dana McGuire owner and operator of
Shenandoah K9 Training
"I'm glad to call you a friend and brother.
Your dedication to your four-legged clients
and your craft are exemplary. Isis has truly
learned from one of the best, thank you."

"What is PTSD?" was written from a child's perspective with the hope of helping children understand what PTSD is, how it affects their loved ones, and to also reassure them that it is not their fault. The situations in this book are only a few examples of what those with PTSD confront on a daily basis.

Born in Harlan County, Kentucky Larry Brandon Burke grew up in Cumberland, Kentucky. He joined the United States Marine Corps on July 27, 1998 and went to boot camp at Paris Island, SC. Brandon left active duty in 2005. He currently lives in Mount Holly, NC with his wife Natasha and their two children, Savannah and Hunter. Brandon is in the picture above with his service dog Isis. Isis and other dogs like her play a large part in helping veterans and service members cope with their PTSD no matter how severe.

Printed in the USA
CPSIA information can be obtained
at www.ICGtesting.com
LVHW020600111123
763660LV00025B/142